Lovable Lucy
Splish Splash Barkyard Bash

Written by Norma E. Roth & Shayna Rose Penn
Illustrated by Adua Hernandez

Lovable Lucy Splish Splash Barkyard Bash
A Book About Friendship
Book Three in the Lovable Lucy Series

Published by Wag Your Tale Press 2023

Text and illustration copyright © 2023 by Lovable Lucy LLC

All rights reserved. No part of this publication, or the characters within it, may be reproduced or distributed in any form or by any means without the prior written consent from the publisher. Permission to reproduce any selection or characters from this book must be requested and granted in writing. Email your permission request to: permissions@lovablelucyseries.com.

Our books may be purchased in bulk, at a discount for educational, promotional or business use. Inquiries can be sent to: sales@lovablelucyseries.com.

Book a Meet the Author event at lovablelucyseries.com or email your request to: events@lovablelucyseries.com.

The illustrations for this book were digitally created.

Illustrations by Adua Hernandez
Book cover and interior design by Adua Hernandez

Library of Congress Control Number: 2022922984

ISBN HC: 978-1-7376630-6-5

Created and designed in the USA
Printed and bound in China

To our Lucy,
for showing us what it means to love
and be a friend to everyone.

Splish splash

My two floppy ears perk up.
I hear the sound of water splashing.
Sara, Remy, and Marlee are filling up our pool.
Mommy and Daddy are setting up picnic tables.

Splish splash

Splish splash

"Lovable Lucy, are you excited for our Barkyard Bash?" asks Sara.

I stare up at Sara.

I wonder, what is a Barkyard Bash?

"Lovable Lucy, we're having a party," says Remy.

"Our friends and their doggies are coming over to play."

I'm excited to see my friends! I run around in a big circle.
"We're going to have tons of fun," squeals Mommy.
"A splishy splashy, fun day," laughs Daddy.

swOOSH

The fence gate swings open.

Our friends are here!

Our friends are excited, too!

Chip runs over to me. Chip barks loudly in my face.
"Chip is extra chipper today," Remy laughs.
"Chip is excited for his first Barkyard Bash."

BARK BARK BARK BARK bark

I want to play with all my friends.
Who should I play with first?

I spy my friend Bagel.
Bagel hides behind Penny's legs.
Bagel's tail hides between her legs.

Uh oh. I know how Bagel feels.
Sometimes my tail hides between my legs, too.

Bagel feels shy.
"It's okay, Bagel," Mommy says. "Sometimes I get shy, too."
I go over to comfort Bagel.
We twitch our noses.
Bagel rubs her nose to mine.

"Lovable Lucy, Bagel appreciates you comforting her," Penny says.
"How are you doing, Bagel?" asks Remy.
Remy pats Bagel's head.
Bagel licks Remy's face.
"Aww, Bagel, that tickles." Remy giggles.

"Bagel, would you like to play frisbee with us?" asks Remy.
Yes! Remy throws the frisbee.

SWOOSH

Bagel and I catch the frisbee.
Bagel feels playful now.

Wag Wag Wag
Wag Wag

Chip feels playful, too.
We invite Chip to play with us.
We chase each other in a big circle.
Bagel and Chip like playing together!

We chase each other to Sara, Sol, and Sammy.
Sammy doesn't play chase with us.
Sammy is "working" right now.
Sammy is Sol's service dog.
Sol is deaf. Sol doesn't hear.
Sammy uses his ears to hear what Sol doesn't hear.
Sammy helps Sol be safe.

Behind Sammy is a big tree.
The tree has a big shadow.
I see the shadow wag its tail.
It's not a shadow, it's my friend Bellow.

I'm excited to see Bellow.
I'm excited to see Bev.
"It's good to see you too, Lovable Lucy," says Bev.
Bellow lets out a big sigh.

Bellow slowly stands up.
Bellow is older than me.
Bellow is bigger than me.
Bellow is so big, I fit under his belly!

Bellow is giant. Bellow is gentle.
Today, Bellow is mellow.
"Lovable Lucy, thank you for spending time with Bellow."
I smile. I like being mellow with my friend Bellow.

My two floppy ears perk up.
I hear Buddy barking.
Buddy is having fun jumping in a puddle.
Buddy is very muddy.

"Lucy, do you want to jump with Buddy?" Tim asks.
"I'll jump with Buddy!" Daddy says.

SQUISH SQUISH

"I'll jump too!" Marlee giggles.
Daddy and Marlee jump in the puddle.
"Wow, Buddy, what a fun idea!"

I want to play with my friend Buddy,
but I don't want to get muddy like Buddy.
I dip my paws in the puddle.

SQUISH SQUISH

My two front paws get
all wet and muddy!

I stare up at Marlee with my big brown eyes.
"Lucy, you turned your white paws brown!"
I spy another puddle. I jump in.

Buddy jumps in the puddle with me.
Buddy and I are best muddy buddies.
"Lovable Lucy, thanks for playing with Buddy," Marlee says.

Chip and Bagel jump in the puddle, too!

Even Bellow jumps in puddles with us!
I like jumping in puddles with my friends.

Sammy jumps, too!

Everyone is splishing.
Everyone is splashing.
Everyone is having fun.

BARK, BARK

Splish splash

We all like jumping together!

Our Barkyard Bash is over.
My friends wave goodbye.
All the doggies wag their tails goodbye.
The yard is quiet without our friends.

Suddenly...

Mommy splashes Daddy. Mommy laughs.
Daddy splashes Mommy. Daddy laughs.
Sara, Remy, and Marlee join the fun.

Splish splash

Splish splash

"I'm all wet," squeals Marlee. "I'm all muddy," laughs Daddy. "I'm all sloppy," says Sara. Remy pauses. "I'm all…loppy!" Everyone laughs.

"Loppy." Mommy rubs Remy's wet head. "That's how I feel, too."

"Lovable Lucy, come play chase!"
Mommy chases me.
I run through the splash mat.
We splish and splash one more time.

"I love our silly family."
"I love our neighborhood friends."

I'm still excited from our Barkyard Bash!
I run all over the backyard.

I run inside the house!
I curl up in my bed. I let out a big yawn.
I'm sleepy from our Barkyard Bash.
Sara rubs my back. Remy rubs my two floppy ears.
Marlee kisses my head.
"Sleep sweetly, Lovable Lucy."

I let out another yawn.
I love comforting my friends.
I love mellowing with my friends.
I even love getting muddy with my friends.
Most of all, I love having all my friends together.

Glossary of Words

Author Note

We are excited to introduce Sara's friend Sol, a Deaf character in "Lovable Lucy Splash Splash Barkyard Bash". Sol is inspired by author Shayna's childhood friend, who is both deaf and has cerebral palsy. At age nine, Shayna took American Sign Language lessons, which allowed her to better communicate with her friend. In these lessons Shayna learned about Deaf culture and how the Deaf community can be misunderstood by the hearing community.

In developing the manuscript and illustrations, we worked with a team of deaf people and educators in the Deaf community. Thank you to Amanda Keeton, Kathleen Larkin, Teagan Nurnberger, Sue Rosenbluth and others who helped us provide the most effective representation of a Deaf character. You can learn more about Sol on our website: www.lovablelucyseries.com.

The dogs in this book are represented without leashes while they're playing with their owners in a backyard space, protected on all sides with a fence boundary.

A leash is the most effective way to keep a dog safe when the dog is outdoors. In most states, when a dog is outdoors, a leash is required. All dog owners should obey their local and state leash laws when bringing their dog outdoors, walking in a neighborhood or visiting a park. One of the best ways to avoid losing a dog, keeping a dog safe from other animals, and keeping people safe from a dog is to keep a dog leashed all the time except in closed/protected boundaries.

Book a Lovable Lucy event for your school or early childhood learning center. Email us: events@lovablelucyseries.com.

Visit lovablelucyseries.com to subscribe to our newsletter, download activities, and connect with us on Instagram: @lovablelucyseries.